The Rooster and His Grandfather

A Rooster was standing on a fence post in a farmer's backyard.

"I know you are not making much money waking the farmer's family," said his Grandfather, resting in the shade of a cherry blossom tree. "But if you work as hard as you can, someday you'll become the richest animal on the farm."

The hardest work the Rooster could think of was digging holes.

Early the next morning, after waking the farmer's family with a hearty "cock-a-doodle-do," the Rooster sharpened his claws on a roll of rusty barbed wire and started digging.

Eager to become the richest animal on the farm, he began scratching deep holes all over the farmer's barnyard and into his orchard.

After hours upon hours of digging, the worn-out Rooster did not get rich. He only got a terrible backache.

Leadership Moral: Work hard but work smart.

The Owl and the Crane

A Crane asked a wise old Owl to look through a folder of oil paintings. The Owl, a well-known artist, shuffled quickly through the artwork and told the Crane the paintings were of little value.

The Crane, accepting the Owl's judgment, pulled out another folder.

"Would you please look through these paintings?" she asked. "They were done by a young art student."

Instantly, the Owl's face lit up with excitement.

"These," he said, "are wonderful! It is obvious this young artist has a bright future in the world of art. She should be encouraged to develop her skills."

At that moment, the Owl could see the Crane was deeply moved.

"Who is this fine artist," he asked, "your daughter?"

"No," the Crane replied with sadness in her voice, "it was me 20 years ago. If only I had heard those encouraging words when I was young, I might have been inspired to further develop my skills."

Leadership Moral: Never underestimate the power of praise.

The Goat Family

A Grandfather Goat went to live with his family. Each night he would sit at the supper table, listening to them tell stories, laugh, and talk about their day.

As he grew older, however, Grandfather became clumsy and had trouble seeing. Eating became very hard for him, and everyone but his Grandson became irritated with the mess he was making.

"We must do something about Grandfather," they said. "We have had enough spilled milk, broken bowls, and food on the floor."

Eventually, they put a mat on the floor in the corner of the kitchen, and Grandfather ate alone while the rest of the family enjoyed dinner together at the table. Sadly, his food was now served in an old wooden bowl.

Quite often, when the Grandson looked at his Grandfather, he could see tears in his eyes, and it made his heart ache. One evening before supper, the Goat Family noticed the Grandson playing on the floor with scraps of wood.

"What are you making?" they asked.

"I am making wooden bowls for all of you to eat from when you grow old like Grandfather."

Leadership Moral: Expect to be treated as you treat others.

The Beaver and the Otter

After a hard day at school, a Beaver was sunning himself near the edge of a freshwater pond.

By chance, a well-dressed Otter stopped and asked how to get to the local post office. The youngster, being an excellent student, gave him detailed directions, and the Otter was very impressed.

"I am a preacher," he said. "If you come to the Water Street Chapel this evening, I will have free tickets for you and your family. I will be telling everyone in your town how to get to Heaven."

"I do not think we will be there," the young Beaver replied. "You don't even know how to get to the post office. Why would anyone believe you could get them to Heaven?"

Leadership Moral: To be a good leader, you must know where you are going.

The Two Turtles

A long time ago, a Painted Turtle and a Snapping Turtle shared a room in a hospital. They were very ill and couldn't leave their beds.

The Painted Turtle was lucky enough to be next to the window. Each day after lunch, he sat up, looked outside, and described a park full of fresh flowers, sparkling streams, and tall, wispy grasses. Thus, the two became close friends.

Before long, the Snapping Turtle thought it unfair his friend could see everything while he could see nothing. Quietly, he became bitter. Late one evening, the Painted Turtle awoke with a fit of coughing and choking and was unable to call the nurse. Sadly, his friend lay silent and did nothing to help. The next morning, the nurse found the Painted Turtle was no longer breathing.

After what seemed to be a proper amount of time, the Snapping Turtle asked if he could move next to the window. It was done, and when the room was empty, he sat up to look outside. To his surprise, the window did not overlook a beautiful park at all. Instead, it faced nothing more than a crumbling, brick wall.

Leadership Moral: Do not jump to negative conclusions.

The Kangaroo, the Mouse, and the Boy

A blind Kangaroo was walking down the sidewalk with the help of a tiny Mouse. When the two came to a busy intersection, the Mouse led the Kangaroo right through traffic.

The Kangaroo had no choice but to follow. The result was complete chaos. Horns beeped, cars swerved, and tires screeched, but somehow the two made it safely to the other side.

Happy to be alive, the frightened Kangaroo reached into his pouch, pulled out a morsel of cheese, and offered it to the reckless Mouse.

Having watched this event unfold, a young Boy approached the Kangaroo.

"Excuse me, sir, your Mouse almost got you run over. Seems to me, the last thing you should do is reward him with a nibble of cheese."

The blind Kangaroo winked and smiled.

"I am not going to give the Mouse this cheese," he whispered. "I am offering it to him so I can find his mouth. Then, I will know where his backside is so I can kick him in the tail."

Leadership Moral: Do not reward negative behavior.

The Seagull and His Lighthouse

A Yellow-legged Seagull became a lighthouse keeper and lived at the end of a long, stone pier. His only job was to keep a fire burning throughout the night to warn sailors.

On his first day, the Seagull received a large barrel of fish oil to help fuel the fire.

Being a friendly bird, visitors flew in to see him quite often. One evening, a Warbler asked for a jug of oil to keep her family warm. On another day, a Wood Duck begged for a cup of oil to keep his lanterns lit. A few days later, a Great Blue Heron pleaded for a small amount to loosen the hinges on his front gate.

In his desire to keep everyone happy, the Seagull never refused a friend. As time passed, favors continued and the barrel was empty. Thus, the lighthouse went dark. That very night, a ship slammed into the pier and many sailors were lost.

When the Coast Guard came to check out the accident, they found the Seagull alone and wandering the beach. Though he was sorry, he tried to make excuses for his actions, but they refused to listen to his squawking.

"Forget the poor excuses," they scolded, "you were given the oil to do one job, keep the fire burning, and you failed."

Leadership Moral: Accept responsibility for your mistakes and refuse to make excuses.

The Tadpole and the Race

A Tadpole woke early each morning to train for a ten-lap race. Though she faced many physical challenges, she was determined to improve her swimming skills and become a champion. After weeks of serious training, her confidence reached a level she had never experienced. When the whistle blew, she leaped from her lily pad into the fresh water and was off to a quick start.

After one lap, the Tadpole was in first place and the crowd started to cheer. Five laps later, she was still in the lead. Inspired by her pace, the fans began chanting her name.

Heading into lap eight, she started to fade and couldn't keep her lead. Sadly, she finished last.

As she crossed the finish line, her name was announced and the crowd stood and cheered. The ovation was heart-warming and sincere.

A Golden-eyed Bullfrog was completely confused by the crowd's reaction. "She finished dead last," she said to a friend standing nearby. "Why is everyone cheering?"

"For a Tadpole who lost most of her tail in a fishing accident, she did quite well, wouldn't you say?"

Leadership Moral: Hard work builds confidence and inspires others to work hard.

The Bullfrog and His Doctor

A Bullfrog, living in a world of cattails and pickle-weed, leaped to a neighboring marsh to see his family Doctor. He was sore from his almond-shaped eyes down to his thin, webbed feet.

"Where do you hurt?" asked the Doctor.

"Doc," the Bullfrog responded with a mournful croak, "everywhere I touch it hurts. When I place my finger on my head it hurts. When I touch my leg it hurts. When I touch my shoulder it hurts."

"Doc," he cried out, "you must help me! Am I going to die?"

"Son, listen to me," the Doctor said as he sat the Frog down on a moss-covered log. "You are not going to die. Your diagnosis is simple. You have a broken index finger."

Leadership Moral: Do not overlook the obvious.

The Prairie Dogs and the Foxes

A group of Prairie Dogs gathered in a secret room to talk about their enemies. A band of hungry Foxes had been attacking them from the North.

After hours of discussion, they decided to build a stone wall around their city.

The tireless Prairie Dogs spent years building a most impressive structure. When it was done, they were all in agreement, their attackers could never charge through or climb over such a magnificent wall.

In the first year, they were invaded three times. Each time, the clever Foxes never busted through or raced over the wall. They simply bribed the gatekeepers and marched right through the gates.

It seems the Prairie Dogs were so busy building walls, they forgot to teach loyalty to their fellow citizens.

Leadership Moral: Teach loyalty first and success is sure to follow.

The Queen of the Cats

In a kingdom on the Isle of Purr, the Queen of the Cats called a meeting with her noble subjects. "Why are we the most successful civilization the world has ever known? There must be an answer. Find it," she pleaded. "Write it down for future generations to study. We must preserve our success." At once, the loyal Cats set out to please their Queen. After two years, they came back with the answer. It consisted of nine thick volumes.

"This is good," the Queen said looking over their work, "but it is much too long. Simplify your findings. I want everyone on this island to be able to understand our success."

The faithful Cats worked day and night for another year and presented the Queen with just one book. She was impressed but encouraged them to simplify more. Ten months later, they shortened their work to just one page. She thanked them and told them she was proud of their commitment but wanted them to keep working. After a few days, the Queen's noble subjects were finally done. This time their answer was just one sentence, and all were in agreement, it would preserve their kingdom forever.

It read: "On the Isle of Purr, every single Cat works hard."

Leadership Moral: To reach team greatness, all must do their part.

24

The Red-winged Blackbird and the Cardinal

A Red-winged Blackbird flew into a castle on the edge of an enchanted forest. He wanted to become a monk.

He understood a monk's promise to be silent, pray for many hours each day, and speak but two words every two years.

With confidence and enthusiasm, the Red-winged Blackbird began his work at once.

After his first two years of silence and prayer, he visited the head Cardinal. Remembering he could only say two words, he sobbed, "Bad bed."

Two years later, he cried out, "Bad food!"

Upon his third visit to the Cardinal, he shouted, "Terrible water!"

Without hesitation, the crazed Blackbird removed his sandals, tore off his robe, and threw them to the Cardinal.

"I quit!" he screamed and headed for the door.

"Praise the Lord!" scolded the troubled Cardinal. "You have done nothing but complain since you arrived!"

Leadership Moral: When times get tough, complainers are sure to quit.

The Pig and the Steamship Owner

A Pot-bellied Pig strolled into the boiler room of a large ship. There was no doubt, he was extremely confident.

"What seems to be the problem with this foul-smelling vessel?" he asked. He was told the main boiler was not working.

The Pig grunted, pulled up his trousers, and swaggered around the room searching for clues. Putting his snout in the air, he proceeded to sniff a few dials and ran his hoof along a couple of steamy pipes. After sitting on his curly tail for a moment, listening to the boiler hiss and thump, he pulled a rubber mallet out of his leather work belt and gently tapped on a bright red valve. The boiler heaved, coughed, sputtered, and began to work perfectly.

A week later, the Steamship Owner received a bill for $2,000. Knowing the Pig stayed only a few minutes, he was furious and demanded a detailed list of all his work. A few days later, he received the following statement:

Tapping with the hammer————— $1.00

Knowing where to tap-------------- $1,999.00

Total --------------------------------- $2,000.00

Leadership Moral: It's hard to put a price tag on experience.

The Penguin, His Teacher, and the Grasshopper

A certain Penguin, being a proud student, spent many hours preparing for his classes. Before his first report card was to be sent home, he was greeted with a surprise quiz. Because the Penguin had breezed through all previous tests and quizzes, he felt confident, on this day, he would do the same. And he did. Until the last question: "What is the first name of the Grasshopper who cleans this room?"

He saw the Grasshopper every morning when he came to class. He knew she worked hard and was friendly, but he never took the time to introduce himself and ask her name.

Regrettably, the young Penguin left the last question blank. Before leaving, one of the students asked the Teacher if the last question counted for their grade.

"Absolutely," he responded, "in your lifetime, you will come across many fine and hard-working individuals. They deserve a warm introduction. The kind gesture will take less than a minute, they will know you care, and it will put more meaning behind a sincere smile, a friendly nod, or a simple hello. Over time, they may even become a close friend, helping you reach your potential."

Leadership Moral: Each new friendship offers opportunity and fulfillment.

The Honey Bee and the Praying Mantis

A Honey Bee was working hard in her flower garden on the other side of the rainbow. A curious Praying Mantis stopped to admire her work.

"My dear Honey Bee," the Mantis said as he adjusted his baseball cap, "you certainly have a wonderful flower garden."

Each row was full of the prettiest flowers the Mantis had ever seen. The border was neatly edged, the plants were perfectly spaced, and the blend of colors was breathtaking.

"My good Bee," he continued, "you are lucky to have such a lovely garden."

"Excuse me, Mr. Mantis," the Honey Bee said, taking off her gloves and wiping the sweat from her brow. "Luck has nothing to do with my garden. It is lovely because I work hard."

Leadership Moral: It takes hard work, not luck, to succeed.

The Caterpillar and His Wife

A Caterpillar rested in the shade of a droopy willow tree. He was sad because his bookstore business was failing.

After weeks of worry and doubt, he decided to set a few goals. Since he had always dreamed of having a bright-red sports car, buying one would be first on his list.

To motivate himself, he took a picture of the exact car he wanted, taped it on his bathroom mirror, and looked at it every morning as he shaved.

Suddenly, the Caterpillar was full of energy. Every day he went to his bookstore early and stayed late. Within a few months, he sold more books than ever before, and he was the happiest little Caterpillar in all the forest.

After a short time, he paid cash for his new car. With a huge smile on his face, he drove home and took his Wife for a ride. She was proud of her husband, and with a twinkle in her eye, she told him so.

The next morning, the Caterpillar rolled out of bed, started to shave, and noticed the picture of the sports car was gone. His Wife had replaced it with a picture of an expensive diamond ring.

Leadership Moral: Goals motivate.

The Porcupine, the Weasel, and Their Teacher

A Porcupine was taking a history test and feeling dishonest. His best friend, a frumpy little Weasel, was looking over his shoulder and copying his answers.

The Porcupine knew it was wrong, but he did not want to lose his friend. So, he let the Weasel cheat.

The next day, the Porcupine got his test back. At the top of his paper was a huge red F, followed by a message in bold print: "You disappoint me very much, Mr. Porcupine. Your answers look exactly like the Weasel's."

To the Porcupine's surprise, his friend got an A. Hoping to save his reputation and improve his grade, he stayed after class to explain what happened.

The Teacher listened to his story and grabbed her grade book.

"In that case, Mr. Porcupine, I will change only the Weasel's grade. He will get an F for cheating. You, sir, will keep your F for allowing him to cheat."

Leadership Moral: Dishonest behavior leads to failure.

The Giraffe and the Fox

A Giraffe woke, wiped the sleep from his bright blue eyes, and stuck his long neck out of his bedroom window. To his surprise, his brand-new truck was missing.

The vehicle had been stolen in the middle of the night by a sly little Fox. The confused Giraffe hurried to put on his slippers, clip-clopped his way to his phone, and called the Police.

They told him they would do their best to find his truck but feared he would never see it again.

Strangely, the vehicle was back in the driveway the next morning. On the front seat were a dozen, sweet-smelling roses, two tickets to the movies, and a note: "I am sorry I took your truck, I had to take my mom to the hospital. Please forgive me and enjoy the movie."

Two nights later, the Giraffe and his Wife put on their finest clothes, jumped in their truck, and went to the theater. When they returned, to their dismay, the Fox had stolen everything in their home.

Leadership Moral: Never trust a stranger.

The Raccoon and the Rabbit

A Raccoon came upon a Rabbit in an art museum. The Rabbit was a world-famous artist.

Introducing herself, the Raccoon begged the Rabbit to paint her picture and offered to pay him a fair sum for his efforts. He agreed, set up his easel, and began painting at once.

Before long, curious bystanders gathered to watch the master at work. After just ten minutes he finished and gave her the painting. It was obvious to everyone watching, she was quite pleased.

Reaching for her purse, she asked the proud Rabbit how much she owed him. He told her the price was five hundred dollars.

"How dare you ask that much!" cried the startled Raccoon. "It only took you ten minutes to paint this picture!"

"My good Raccoon," the Rabbit responded, "do not offend me. It took a lifetime to master the skills needed to paint this picture."

Leadership Moral: The rewards for mastering one's talents are plentiful.

The Hamster and the Guns of War

A Hamster hopped on his motor scooter and headed for the ocean. He was joining the Navy. He told his friends he was going to help his country win the war, and they shook with laughter. After basic training, he was assigned to work in the kitchen of a submarine. As he wanted to do more for his country, he felt useless. While cleaning tables one evening, he overheard his Captain and five officers planning the largest invasion of the war. They wanted to land heavy equipment on an enemy beach, but they did not know if the sand was firm enough to do so.

The next morning, the Hamster went to see his Captain and told him he had an idea that might help. To everyone's surprise, the Hamster's daring plan was accepted. That night, the sub eased up out of the water, the Hamster climbed into a tiny rubber raft, and quietly rowed toward the beach.

With huge enemy guns overhead, he reached shore, grabbed a handful of sand, and headed back to the sub. The next day the sand was tested and proved firm enough to hold heavy equipment. The invasion was launched, the war was won, and the Hamster became a national hero.

Leadership Moral: Everyone can make a difference.

The Angelfish and the Tiger Shark

An Angelfish, swimming in a sea of sunken ships and lost treasures, was feeling sorry for himself. His classmates made fun of him, and he had no friends. After years of heartache, he decided to run away.

When his parents went to bed, he quietly floated out the back door and headed for the unknown. When he came upon a magnificent coral reef, he searched its shallow waters for a place to live. As he swam, he became confused. Life inside the reef was calm, pale, and lazy, while life outside the reef was bright, vibrant, and full of action. He asked a Tiger Shark why it was so different.

"The open sea pounds and challenges life outside the reef. To survive, all living things must fight back with spirit and enthusiasm. The results, as you can see, are beautiful. Though life inside the reef is free of trouble, there is no sense of accomplishment. Thus, everything becomes dull and lifeless."

Moving closer to the young Angelfish, he whispered, "Do not run away from your troubles, run toward them."

Realizing the Tiger Shark was giving him good advice, the Angelfish thanked him and confidently swam home.

Leadership Moral: Challenges help build confidence and develop character.

The Bear, the Starfish, and the Raven

A Brown Bear was walking along a hidden beach littered with stranded Starfish. The Bear was picking them up with her large paws and gently tossing them back into the sea.

A Raven happened by and was puzzled by what he saw.

"My good friend, what are you doing?" asked the Raven as he approached the Bear.

"It is low tide," the Bear answered politely, "these Starfish will die if I do not get them back into the water."

"I see," said the Raven, "but there are thousands upon thousands of Starfish on this beach. Don't you understand, there are so many you can't possibly make a difference?"

The Bear shook her head, picked up another Starfish, and carefully tossed it back into the sea.

Looking over her shoulder toward the Raven, with a wink and a smile she said, "Made a difference to that one, wouldn't you say?"

Leadership Moral: We can make a difference, one step at a time.

The Mule, the Ram, and the Shepherd Boy

A Ram was leading a Pack Mule across a gravel road when the Mule decided to stop and sit down. They had traveled many miles without rest, and the Mule's load of corn and grain had become a burden.

The Ram became furious and scolded the Mule, but he refused to budge. In frustration, the Ram moved behind the Mule, put his horns against his back, and began to push. The weary Mule dug his hooves into the gravel, stiffened his front legs, and pressed back against the Ram.

The angry Ram quit pushing, grabbed a large stick, and prepared to strike the Mule. At that moment a Shepherd Boy happened by and begged him to stop.

The Boy pulled an apple out of his backpack, rubbed it until it shined, and handed it to the worn-out Mule.

As the Mule nibbled the apple, the Boy stroked his mane and whispered softly in his ear. When the Mule finished, the Shepherd Boy gently tugged on his guide rope. The Mule rose, stretched his legs, and continued carrying his load down the gravel road.

Leadership Moral: Kindness has a positive impact on others.

The Cricket and the Three-toed Sloth

A Cricket was taking his two daughters to the circus. They were excited to watch the Elephants walk on two legs. As they moved in line to buy their tickets, they heard a Hippopotamus shouting into a megaphone: "Hurry! Hurry! Step right up! See the circus animals in all their splendor. Only two dollars a ticket! Those under the age of two get in free!"

One of the young Crickets had just turned two. The other was a bit older. When it was their father's turn to pay, he gave the Three-toed Sloth in the ticket booth six dollars.

"Here are two dollars for my ticket and two for each of my daughters."

The Sloth counted the money and slowly placed it in the cash register. He tilted his head and looked over his glasses at the two young Crickets.

"My good Cricket," he said, "you could have saved four dollars. I never would have known your daughters are over the age of two."

"Yes, that may be true," the proud father responded, "but my daughters would have known, and I want to teach them to be fair and honest."

Leadership Moral: Honesty is always the best policy.

The Goldfinch and Miss Bluebird

A Goldfinch sat down to write a letter to one of his teachers. Her name was Miss Bluebird. She gave him confidence and made him believe his dreams could come true. With her help, he became one of the most successful Birds in all the meadows and orchards. One week after sending the letter, he received a return letter:

My dear Goldfinch,

I want you to know what your note meant to me. I am an old Bluebird, now in my eighties. I live alone, cooking my own meals and feeling like the last leaf on a tree. I taught school for fifty years. In all that time, yours is the first letter of thanks I have ever received. It came on a cold, cloudy day, and it cheered my lonely heart as nothing has cheered me in many years.

Your teacher,
Miss Bluebird

The Goldfinch's letter took only a few minutes to write. Yet, it was enough to make the Bluebird happy.

Leadership Moral: A simple thank you may bring joy and happiness.

The Parrot

A lonely Parrot had a terrible childhood. Before she was three years old, she lost her parents and was raised by relatives who treated her poorly.

Making life even tougher, she was painfully shy, had a terrible speech problem, and her classmates made fun of the way she talked.

Longing to fit in, the sad Parrot would try anything to overcome her speaking problems. She practiced talking with pebbles in her mouth, sang songs into the wind, and tried reciting poems in a single breath.

Though improving her speech was extremely difficult, she succeeded. She grew up, had many friends, and became a famous public speaker. Over time, she was called by some the "most perfect speech-giver in all the land."

Leadership Moral: Be determined to turn weakness into strength.

The Pelican and the Butterfly

A Pelican, walking through a warm field of sunflowers and buttercups, found the cocoon of a Butterfly. Moving closer, he noticed a tiny opening at one end.

Peeking inside, he watched the Butterfly struggling to get out and decided to help. With his pouch-like beak, he made the hole much bigger and watched the tiny Butterfly come out without a struggle.

To the Pelican's surprise, the Butterfly's body was swollen. Looking closer, he noticed her wings were shriveled and wouldn't open.

The poor Butterfly never flew, spending the rest of her life crawling.

What the Pelican did not know was the importance of a Butterfly's struggle. Fighting to get through the small opening of a cocoon, fluid is forced throughout their wings, making them strong enough to fly.

Leadership Moral: Struggle can be a stepping-stone to growth and development.

The Honey Badger

A Honey Badger was a great athlete and had strong legs and a solid build. Though he was short, he could run faster and jump higher than all his friends. Thus, he gave hope to other small Badgers who wanted to be good athletes.

One cold and rainy night, the Badger was injured in a terrible car accident. For the rest of his life, he would not be able to move his arms or his legs. Though many of his hopes and dreams were shattered, he did not feel sorry for himself or get mad at the world. Refusing to give up on life, he decided to become a painter. Badgers throughout the animal kingdom were confused. How would he be able to paint?

Working hard each day, the Honey Badger found a way. His Nurse dipped his brush in the paint and placed the handle in his mouth. With his teeth, his tongue, and his lips, he moved the brush.

After months and months of hard work, his first painting was complete, and it was spectacular. What did the Badger paint? Wanting to inspire, he used bright reds, yellows, and greens and painted a beautiful picture of a smiling clown.

When his friends saw his inspiring work they all agreed, he was the most amazing Honey Badger they had ever known.

Leadership Moral: Tough times offer opportunities to inspire.

The Army Ants and Their Leader

Thirty Army Ants tumbled out of their bunk beds and hurried to get dressed in their regular Army uniforms. When they finished, with legs kicking and heads bobbing, they hustled out the door and were met by their fearless Leader.

"Okay Ants," the gravel-voiced Leader shouted, "let's try this again! You have exactly two minutes to hustle back to your barracks, change into your full-dress uniforms, and get back out here!"

It didn't matter how hard they tried, two minutes seemed impossible to change from one uniform to the other. But when their Leader yelled, "Dismissed!" they scurried back to their rooms and started changing. When finished, each tumbled out the door until the last ones ended up in the late line.

"Why are you late, mister?" the Leader called out to one of the tardy Ants.

"There is no excuse, sir!"

"That's right, there is no excuse! If one of you is late, all of you are late. If you Ants would work together, as a team, you might make it out here in time."

Late that night, they helped each other tie their shoes, buckle their belts, and button their shirts. Over and over they practiced until they were at their best.

When the next order came to change uniforms, they hurried back to their rooms, worked together, and didn't leave until all were ready. And because they practiced as a team, they returned in full-dress uniform in two minutes!

Leadership Moral: With teamwork, all things are possible.

Fun facts about the characters in Fables for Young Leaders, the First Step

The Butterfly and the Ladybug
Butterflies use their feet to taste.
Ladybugs bleed from their knees when threatened.

The Rooster and His Grandfather
Roosters dream when they sleep.

The Owl and the Crane
Owls have super-powered hearing.
Cranes can fly as high as 13,000 feet.

The Goat Family
Goats can be taught their name and will come when called.

The Beaver and the Otter
The beaver is Canada's national symbol.
Otters use rocks to break open clams.

The Two Turtles
A painted turtle's skin color looks like an artist painted it on.
A snapping turtle has a stronger force bite than an alligator.

The Kangaroo, the Mouse, and the Boy

Most kangaroos are left-handed. Mice eat between 15 and 20 times a day.

The Seagull and His Lighthouse

Seagulls will turn away when you make contact with them. Warblers are so small, they've been known to get caught in spider webs.

The Tadpole and the Race

Tadpoles drink water through their skin. Male bullfrogs have yellow throats; females have white.

The Bullfrog and His Doctor

Bullfrogs do not have teeth and use their large eyeballs to push food down their throat. Goldfish can live to be 40 years old.

The Prairie Dogs and the Foxes

Prairie dogs have specific calls for different enemies, including one for a human with a gun. A fox is more like a cat than a dog, can climb trees, and retract its claws.

The Queen of the Cats

Cats have 18 toes. There are over 500 million pet cats.

The Red-winged Blackbird and the Cardinal

At times, over 1 million blackbirds settle at night in a single area. Because of their beautiful colors, cardinals are a reminder that loved ones will never truly be forgotten.

The Pig and the Steamship Owner

Pot-bellied pigs and dogs get along, but for the pig's sake, should never be left alone.

The Penguin, His Teacher, and The Grasshopper

Penguins are flightless birds and live exclusively in the Southern Hemisphere. Grasshoppers have ears on their bellies and rub their legs together to make musical sounds.

The Honey Bee and the Praying Mantis

Female honey bees are the only type of bee to have stingers and are the only type of bee that dies after stinging. Praying mantis can turn their heads 180 degrees.

The Caterpillar and His Wife

A caterpillar's only job is to eat, and they have over 4,000 muscles.

The Porcupine, the Weasel, and Their Teacher

Porcupines can have 30,000 quills, used to fight infections. Weasels have long whiskers on their tails to help them crawl.

The Giraffe and the Fox

Giraffes hum, have three hearts, and three brains.

Foxes are smelly, live in underground dens, and can make 40 different sounds.

The Raccoon and the Rabbit

Raccoons love life in big cities but fear people. A rabbit's teeth never stop growing. When happy, they twist and kick in mid-air.

The Hamster and the Guns of War

Hamsters are intelligent creatures and can learn their name.

The Angelfish and the Tiger Shark

Angelfish are shy and like to hide behind plants and rocks. Tiger sharks do not have bones and are known to eat anything, including other sharks.

The Bear, the Starfish, and the Raven

Some bears build nests in trees. Starfish have no brain and no blood. A raven's call can be heard up to one mile away.

The Mule, the Ram, and the Shepherd Boy

It is believed there are 15 million mules in the world. Rams have a split in their upper lip to help pick the leaves they prefer.

The Cricket and the Three-toed Sloth

In parts of the world, people love to eat crickets. They weigh less than one paperclip. Three-toed sloths are the slowest mammals in the world but are graceful swimmers.

The Goldfinch and Miss Bluebird

To stay warm at night, some goldfinch burrow under the snow to make a cozy place to sleep. A bluebird can spot caterpillars in tall grass from over 50 yards away.

The Parrot

Parrots taste with the tops of their beaks. One African-gray parrot named Alex was able to speak more than 100 words.

The Pelican and the Butterfly

The beak of an Australian Pelican is the largest of all birds. They swing the pouch below their beak to cool off. Butterfly wings are covered by thousands of tiny scales that reflect different colors.

The Honey Badger

Honey Badgers are mean, hard to kill, and sleep in the dens of other animals.

The Army Ants and Their Leader

A swarm of army ants can kill 100,000 insects in a single day.

Fable Sources

The Butterfly and the Ladybug
What Makes the Great Great, Dennis Kimbro

The Rooster and His Grandfather
Developing the Leader Within You, John C. Maxwell

The Owl and the Crane
What Makes the Great Great, Dr. Dennis Kimbro

The Goat Family
Host of The Mindfulness Summit, Melli O'Brien

The Beaver and the Otter
Developing the Leader Within You, John C. Maxwell

The Two Turtles
Developing the Leader Within You, John C. Maxwell

The Kangaroo, the Mouse, and the Boy
Winning Every Day, Lou Holt

The Seagull and His Lighthouse
Developing the Leader Within You, John C. Maxwell

The Porcupine, the Weasel, and Their Teacher

Anonymous"The Giraffe and the Fox" - Anonymous

The Raccoon and the Rabbit

The Rhythm of Life, Matthew Kelly

The Hamster and the Guns of War

Anonymous

The Angelfish and the Tiger Shark

The Psychology of Winning, Dr. Dennis Waitley

The Bear, the Starfish, and the Raven

Chicken Soup for the Soul

The Mule, the Ram, and the Shepherd Boy

Chicken Soup for the Soul

The Cricket and the Three-toed Sloth

Chicken Soup for the Soul

The Goldfinch and Miss Bluebird

Table Talk for Family Fun, Martin Buxbaum

The Parrot
On the Crown, Professor James J. Murphy

The Pelican and the Butterfly
Benefits of Struggle in Life, Dr. Rekha Ramankutty

The Honey Badger
To Lead a Good Life, Tony Legando

The Army Ants and Their Leader
Leading with the Heart, Mike Krzyzewski

About the Author

Tony Legando was born in Huron, Ohio. He graduated from Huron High School and received a Bachelor of Science in Education from Ashland University. He taught elementary school for 40 years, was the head football coach for 28 years, and is a member of the Ohio High School Football Coaches Association Hall of Fame.

Tony lives in Huron with his wife Sandy. He has two children, Tony and Jessie Gimperling, granddaughters, Rece and Layne Gimperling, and Fionna Balzer.

Tony is a team-building specialist who has influenced leaders throughout his professional career and has taken his passion to mentor, impact and facilitate on the road as a motivational speaker.

Tony writes a column in the *Sandusky Register* and their affiliate newspapers throughout North Central Ohio. *Fables for Young Leaders, the First Step* is his second book. His first, *To Lead a Good Life*, is a self-help book highlighting 62 motivational stories, inspirational essays, and lessons on effective leadership. It was published in September 2020.

About the Illustrator

Darcy Berardi is from Maumee, Ohio, and currently lives in Huron, Ohio. She received a Bachelor of Science in Art Education from Bowling Green State University. Darcy continues to teach private Art lessons and wine and canvas paint parties. She has an Art business that includes murals, portrait drawing, painted furniture, and jewelry making.

She feels life is short, but Art lives forever. You can contact Darcy at dberardi1229@gmail.com.

Note to parents, grandparents, teachers, coaches, guardians, and relatives:

It was my pleasure writing *Fables for Young Leaders, the First Step*. As I'm proud of this book and the lessons it offers, I want to share it with as many potential leaders as possible. It would be much appreciated if you'd take the time to write a short review and submit it to Amazon.com.

If you'd like to know more about my leadership journey, check out my website at tonylegando.com, read my first book, *To Lead a Good Life*, or contact me at legandot@gmail.com.

Made in the USA
Monee, IL
24 February 2023

27840496R20046